Copyright

Introduction

The purpose of this guide is to allow ANYONE to ace an investment banking, hedge fund or private equity interview by influencing your appearance, attitude, mindset, behavior and actual answers.

If you've taken some finance classes or have experience in finance, I hope that you understand some of the in-depth finance discussions. Regardless of your background, remember that none of this stuff is rocket science. I went to one of the best undergraduate business / finance programs in the country but was a HORRIBLE analyst for the first 3-4 months. But it doesn't matter, all the finance explained here can be learned. And once you have a job, you will be given at least 6 months to learn as long as you show up to work and show that you're eager to improve.

Do not get discouraged if you do not understand any of the finance discussed in this guide. Try your best to understand it, try your best to memorize or get familiar with the concepts, but, most importantly, make sure that you modify your behavior to EXACTLY the person that we're looking to hire.

Most Investment Bankers only last ~2-3 years, maximum, in the industry. They usually end up quitting because the stress is too high. Therefore, it's imperative to not show any weakness during the interview. You must convey a commitment to excellence and portray an image of an "efficient perfectionist" in everything you produce. You must also portray unwavering loyalty to the position and the importance of getting things done regardless of circumstances.

Whether you actually carry these feelings with you after a month, or two, on the job is another story. But it's always good to have options. And the best way to land the job is to play the card that if you're provided with an opportunity, you will exceed expectations.

How to Get Interviews

As bankers, we're concerned about the candidates' work ethic. We work a lot of hours, (about 80-100/week) and we need to know that you can do the job and produce a high quality work product.

As such, combined with a keen interest in finance, you need to show the interviewer that you can produce a high-quality work product.

In preparation for the interview you need to **show us that you can DO the job AND that you're excited at the possibility of being an analyst. A genuine passion combined with technical proficiency will land you a job.**

A few examples of demonstrating this is:

- Show an interest in finance – take finance classes in college and/or show us that you're interested in the stock market.

- Show that you're a hard worker – that you have spent hours in the library studying for exams. That you were a part of numerous teams/organizations in college, etc.

- Grades are also very important as well! Try to have a **3.5 GPA** or better. This will help you obtain an interview. I remember my Director dumping stacks of resumes on all the Analysts at 11pm, while we were all busy with other work, and asking us to sort them into "2 piles". We spent 5-10 seconds per resume and pretty-much sorted based on GPA.

- Be smart – we like to see people who are intelligent. This job is not rocket science, and much of the terminology is used primarily to separate and create an appearance of exclusivity between those who understand and those who do not. However you will have to remember multiples: LTM ("last twelve months") EBITDA numbers and recent precedent transaction multiples. So we'd like to know that you can remember and apply these figures.

- You also must be able to multi-task and handle enormous amounts of stress. Contrary to what many people will tell you, the hours are not the worst part of the job, rather it's the stress. I have gotten physically sick numerous times from the enormous levels of stress in my job. Each individual copes in different ways, however you DO get better at handling the anxiety with experience.

- **Bonus points if you're really good with Excel. Can write macros and also if you're a math whiz.**

- **We also have to like you. If you're too loud and/or obnoxious, then you'll get dinged because no one will want to work with you.**

Prior to answering interview questions, what's the best way to actually get an interview?

The easiest way is via on-campus recruiting. Befriend and utilize your on-campus recruiters. It's their job to get you a job. Job placement makes their college / University look good and they're highly motivated to place you in the best position possible.

Additionally, you can look at job sites like Monster.com / Vault.com / Indeed.com / Simplyhired.com , etc.

For more experienced hires, a headhunter can be used. Glocap.com, Bondstreetgroup.com etc are examples.

You can also contact firms directly on their website or even contact the CEO or head of HR directly. For example, you can "derive" an email address by finding out the typical format a firm uses. Most use *first.lastname@website.com* or *firstinitial.lastname@website.com* – then you can send a BRIEF email to the contact person, with your resume attached, and state that you're an incredibly hard worker and am looking for an opportunity to prove yourself and exceed expectations.

I actually used this last strategy and got amazing results. An actual email I've used, and had success with, is below:

-----Original Message-----
From: David Jaffee [mailto:d_____mail.com]
Sent: Monday, January 01, 200_ 8:01 AM
To: S_____
Subject: David Jaffee Resume

I'd like to see if there are any open associate positions at your firm.

I'm results-oriented, honest and upfront and also an extremely hardworker that is committed to success.

If the right position presents itself, then I'd simply like the opportunity to show you that I produce good work and be a valuable member of the team.

Attached is my resume.

Best regards,

David

Acing the Interview

Suggested Answers to Interview Questions

Here are some suggested answers to some commonly asked questions:

1) How should I act/speak during the interview?

You should be yourself during the interview. Don't be too uptight and don't try to be too over-the-top professional (it may come off as arrogant). Be yourself and be comfortable. Your goal is to make the person across the table like you. **The best way to do that is to have confidence that you can do the job well.** Don't act conceited or think that you know it all. All you have to do is make the person believe that you're an OCD perfectionist, pay close attention to detail and that you're willing to give up your youth to make sure that each document you produce has zero mistakes.

2) Why do you want to work here? (Fit question)

DO NOT SAY THAT YOU WANT TO WORK THE HOURS – this is BS and we assume you're lying. The best response is, "From the people I've met and spoken to I feel that I would fit in very well. Everyone is very intelligent, driven, hardworking and competitive, however they're also very nice and easy to talk to. I'm also very hardworking and driven. I realize that our goal here is to get as much work done as possible so that we can help originate business for the firm and I can see myself working hard alongside the people I've met. All I want is the opportunity to do good work, and I truly feel that I can accomplish that here."

3) Do you have other offers?

The best response is, "Yes, I have been fortunate enough to receive other offers."

The next question that they will likely ask is, "From who?" or "From what type of companies?" The best response is, if you're interviewing with an investment bank, "From a few other investment banks. For confidentiality reasons, I do not wish to disclose the names, yet I have really been impressed with everyone I have met here so far."

If it's a hedge fund, the answer is similar "From a few other hedge funds. For confidentiality reasons, I do not wish to disclose the names....."

This is the best response because it validates their interest in you. If you accepted their offer, they would not only hire a great person, but they would "steal" an analyst from their competitors.

You can also say, more explicitly, that you have offers from their direct competitors and will evaluate each opportunity at the end of the process, but that you have met some incredible people so far at this company and am excited about the opportunity.

4) What is investment banking?

Investment banking provides companies, governments and institutions with the ability to execute their goals. We facilitate transactions by acting as intermediates between institutions and the capital markets. If a company wants to raise money, then they will come to us to access the equity and/or debt markets. If they want to restructure their debt, then they will come to us as well. If they want to purchase another company and pursue a merger, sale or an acquisition then they will come to us. Basically, we possess the ability and network that allows companies to carry out their financial goals. As such, we're providing a service.

As analysts, you can expect to prepare a lot of pitches. In a pitchbook, we'll tell the Company what service we can provide them. Typically, we'll include credentials that will establish us as the best bank for that company, then we'll include our assessment of the market and the company's position in the marketplace; finally we'll propose an idea and justification for our thoughts outlining the benefits of mandating, and paying, us for our ideas and execution of the transaction. We're typically engaged on a monthly retainer + expenses. Retainers typically run around $50,000 a month and then we're reimbursed for dinners, creative work, printing and travel expenses related to that deal. The real money comes at closing time, where we get about 2%-7% of a multi-million (oftentimes over $100 million) dollar transaction.

We'll also work on various memos such as credit, due diligence and commitment committee memos.

5) Why do you want to do Investment Banking?

Answer as follows: "I've always been interested in finance. Even at a young age I was interested in why stocks trade at the levels that they do. Going through college, I became more interested in the subject and I figure that banking is the best way to **learn as much as possible in a short period of time.** I know it's hard work, that I'll work 100 hours/week, however everything that I've done, I've strived to do well and I will have no problems working the hours because I will be learning a tremendous amount in the process."

Be sure to work in the fact that you produce a high quality work product. Say things such as, "I've always taken pride in the quality of my work product and I would embrace the possibility of becoming an integral member of the team. My work is like my signature and I want my superiors to request me on their deal teams."

6) Can You Negotiate a Larger Signing Bonus After Receiving An Offer?

Yes, I was actually able to do this. After speaking with friends around campus, I realized that the average signing bonus was $7,500 - $15,000. If your initial offer contains a signing bonus that you believe can be increased, your best bet is to call Human Resources and say, "Hey. I'm really interested in accepting your offer. I really like the people and believe that I would add a lot of value there. The issue is that I have other offers with higher signing bonuses. And a bunch of my friends have offers with signing bonuses of $15,000, yet [insert company name] is offering $xxx,xxx. I'd like to commit to 'Insert Bank Name' and accept the offer if they're willing to commit to me as well. What are your thoughts?"

In my case, the HR lady said, "I don't think that will be a problem." She then said she would call me back within 10 minutes. When she did, I was able to secure a 100% increase in my signing bonus.

Basically, you want to make it sound like you have multiple offers and that you are willing to choose this bank, over their competitors, as long as they're willing to match the upper-range of the signing bonuses that are offered.

7) How do you calculate Enterprise Value and what is it?

Enterprise value is the minimum value for which a company can be bought. We typically calculate it by taking:

Market Value of Equity + Book Value of Debt + Minority Interest + Preferred Equity – Cash and Marketable Securities.

The more basic, and common, definition is Market Value of Equity + Debt – Cash.

There is intuition behind this. The Market Value of Equity (current stock prices * shares outstanding) + Debt is the minimum you'd have to pay to buy the company and satisfy the equity and debt holders. We subtract cash because it's not currently part of the operating income of the business and it's already been generated. If I'm buying a wallet, I can pay you for what the wallet is worth, or you can place a $10 dollar bill inside the wallet – in which case I'll have to pay the cost of the wallet + $10. We like to keep things simple, so we subtract cash and marketable securities (things that can be liquidated at a moments notice such as stocks, bonds and derivatives).

In an M&A transaction, there is also significant discussions regarding working capital and how much needs to be left in the business versus how much can be liquidated. This is oftentimes negotiated after an offer has been extended yet before closing (more on this later on).

8) What is EBITDA?

EBITDA is defined as Earnings before Interest, Taxes, Depreciation and Amortization. We use EBITDA because it's a surrogate for cash flow and is very easy to calculate. It mitigates a company's capitalization structure (amount of debt on their balance sheet) by taking earnings before interest expense.

EBITDA is found by adding D&A from the **cash flow statement** to EBIT (operating income) on the income statement. EBIT is defined as Gross Margin – Operating Expenses and is commonly referred to as Operating Income.

We typically use Adjusted EBITDA, which "adds back" non-recurring and non-operating expenses that are contained in Cost of Goods Sold and/or Selling, General and Administrative expenses ("SG&A") . For example, if the Company places "Gain/Loss on the Sale of an Asset" as a line item contained in their SG&A, then this expense would alter the Company's Operating Income (EBIT). However, the Company is not in the business of selling assets, so we would "add-back" (essentially reverse) the charge (or negate the gain) so that Adjusted EBITDA is reflective of the Company's true operating activities.

Usually multiples are calculated using Adjusted EBITDA and any adjustments in the calculation of Adjusted EBITDA are referenced as footnotes.

9) How do you define Free Cash Flow?

Free cash flow is EBIT*(1-Tax Rate "T") + Depreciation and Amortization (on the cash flow statement) – Capital Expenditures – Increase in Net Working Capital.

Or, much more common, Operating cash flow – Capital Expenditures

Typically, the easiest method is to take the Operating Cash Flow (found on the cash flow statement) and subtract Capital Expenditures (also found on the cash flow statement in the Cash Flow from Investments section). However, the first definition is also useful because it shows how to calculate cash flow from EBIT.

Net Working Capital ("NWC") is the summation of inventories, accounts receivables, accounts payable, etc. It's basically the capital that you need to run your business. If your NWC increases, then you've USED cash (such as increasing your inventory). If your NWC decreases, then you've INCREASED your cash flow (such as decreased inventory and/or decreased your accounts receivables and collected cash).

Net working capital can also be defined as Current Assets – Current Liabilities. If someone asks you what working capital is, merely say, "It is the goods needed to run the business, composed of current assets and current liabilities such as inventory, receivables, payables, accrued expenses, etc."

Go to a large department store such as Filenes and sit in their shoe department – as I did with my mother on Labor Day weekend in 2004 – while she was trying everything on I marveled at how many shoes they had in inventory. If Filenes were to increase their inventory, they'd have to buy more shoes and spend cash in the process. If their inventory decreased, then they sold more shoes and their cash flow increased.

10) What is a DCF (discounted cash flow) analysis?

DCF values the Enterprise value of a company based upon its expected future cash flows. You calculate a DCF by dividing the present value of future cash flows by WACC.

11) How do you calculate WACC?

Use the Capital Asset Pricing Model (CAPM) to calculate your cost of equity. This is simply, the **risk free rate + (beta * market risk premium)**

Typically, the risk free rate is just the 10-year treasury rate. Beta (for the individual stock) is found on Yahoo or Bloomberg. The equity risk premium (or market risk premium) is typically about 4% and it's defined as the return of a benchmark, such as the S&P 500 minus the risk-free rate.

The debt component of WACC is computed by taking the weighted average interest rate of the company's existing debt and multiplying it by (1-T). This is because you realize a tax shield whenever debt is issued. Meaning that if you did not pay that money in interest, then it would be counted as income, but since you get taxed on income, then you'd only realize that income * (1-T) to your bottom line. Since interest expense reduces your taxable net income, the "real" affect of the interest expense on your bottom line, if it were counted as income, is interest expense * (1-T). So when we calculate WACC, we take the interest rate * (1-T).

WACC is computed by taking the weighted average cost of both the debt and equity components. It's typically in the range of 10-12%.

The appropriate rate for discounting the company's cash flow stream is the weighted average of the costs of debt and equity capital. For example, if a company's after tax cost of debt is 6% and its estimated cost of equity is 16% and it utilizes 20% debt and 80% equity, it computes the cost of capital at 14% as follows:

	Weight	Cost	Weighted Cost
Debt	20%	6%	1.2%
Equity	80%	16%	12.8%
Cost of Capital			14.0%

To complete your DCF analysis. You would use a terminal value once the company has reached a steady state (where their D&A is equal to their Capital Expenditures) and it's typically a multiple of (6X-8X) their LTM (Last Twelve Months) or last projected year's EBITDA.

We rarely ever use DCF models. I've been doing banking for almost 2 years and have done ONE DCF model. It's NEVER used as the sole means of valuation because it's so unreliable. It relies too heavily on projected cash flows and is rarely accurate. Sometimes we'll use it to support our comparable company analysis valuation, but that's about it. The reason is that it relies upon projections far too heavily, instead of historical numbers. Plus, DCF analysis can easily be manipulated. In short, I did more DCF analysis in college than I did in the "real world".

12) Why do we use multiples?

We use multiples to see how the market is valuing, and has valued, companies. Typically we value off of Enterprise Value / Last Twelve Months EBITDA numbers.

The EV/ LTM EBITDA multiples vary by industry, current state of the economy and also the demand for the company.

Many M&A and LBO transactions are priced off LTM EBITDA numbers

13) What is leverage?

Leverage refers to the amount of debt the company has on its balance sheet. We typically look at debt as a multiple of Total Debt/LTM EBITDA. The ideal multiple is dependent on the industry, current economy and the inherent cyclical nature of the industry. As a general rule, anything above 2.5x-3.0x is considered high.

If a company is highly levered and carries a lot of debt then 2 things happen. First, net income is directly decreased due to the interest expense associated with the debt. Second, owning equity becomes more risky. Therefore, equity holders will demand a higher return, which usually translates into a lower stock price (and lower equity valuation or PE multiple).

Think about it logically. If I owe $1.0 million dollars and ask you to lend me $100,000 you are going to be very hesitant and will likely charge me an absurd amount of interest. However if I have $5.0 million in the bank, then you will charge me a lower rate and feel a lot more comfortable extending the loan to me.

It's the same thing in the stock market. **INCREASED LEVERAGE TYPICALLY LEADS TO LOWER EQUITY VALUATIONS.** This is attributed to the increased likelihood that the company will go bankrupt, lower net income due to the interest expense being paid on the debt and **also the higher interest rate that creditor's will charge on each additional dollar of debt that the Company wants to borrow.** Investors want to know that the company is reinvesting capital into the business to fuel growth, however if the company is already saddled with large amounts of debt, then it will be less likely to borrow money to pursue mergers and acquisitions, complete share buybacks, pay dividends and / or restructure its debt.

14) How do the 3 major financial statements link together?

This is a common question.

The net income line is the top line of the cash flow statement and also has a direct impact, along with shareholder distributions, on the Retained Earnings account on the balance sheet. The Net Income line item encompasses the entire income statement, whereas the cash flow statement merely adjusts net income for the changes in cash. For example, if my accounts receivables increase by $5 billion dollars and I had $6 billion in sales for the quarter, then I've booked $6 billion in sales on my income statement, but I haven't received $5 billion of it in cash yet.

15) How do interest rates affect the market?

You likely won't be asked this. I would probably ask someone this if they seemed extremely cocky because I would want to see if they had any idea how interest rates affect the market.

Okay. The answer is: It affects the market in multiple ways.

Increased interest rates increase the "risk free rate". As a result, investors will require a higher return on equity. Some investors will believe that equity will not be able to return enough to justify their investment, so they'll take money out of the market, and thus decrease demand for stocks. This will lead to lower stock prices and valuations. Basically, an increase in interest rates increases the competition for money away from the stock market. It's sort of like, "Why would I invest in the market when I can earn XX% just by keeping money in my savings account?"

This is also the intuition behind the CAPM formula. If the risk-free rate goes up, then your required return on equity will increase (assuming a reasonable beta and a constant market risk premium)

Interest rates also increase the cost of borrowing for corporations. Therefore, companies are less likely to invest in growth projects that will add future shareholder value. They'll wait for rates to decrease, and then borrow, prior to undertaking a huge capital expenditure.

Rising interest rates also increase the attractiveness of bonds – which compete with equity for investor's cash.

Increased interest rates decrease the prices of all existing debt currently in the market. If I have a piece of debt that pays me $50 for every $1000, and then rates are raised so that new debt will pay me $60 for every $1000. My original debt piece will drop down to $833 in order to balance out the yields – 60/1000 = 6%, 50/833 = 6%.

There are a few more things about rates, such as their effect on existing yields and their affect on the convexity and duration of the yield curve, however I wouldn't worry about this at all.

16) What is the difference between a capital and operating lease?

When something is capitalized, it is placed on the balance sheet ("BS"). An operating lease is an off-balance sheet account (because it does not show up on the BS). Rather, it shows up on the income statement as Rent Expense or whatever else they want to call it. However, we sometimes treat operating leases as debt because they represent future obligations. So, we would take 8x the last twelve month's rent expense and add this to the Company's total debt. Sometimes we do this, sometimes we don't. It depends on what we're looking to show and the exact circumstance.

17) Is this deal accretive or dilutive?

Look at the PE ratios of both the target and the acquirer. If the target's PE ratio is **lower** than the acquirer's then the deal is **accretive.** Under no circumstances are acquirers willing to accept acquisitions which are permanently dilutive. If the market is valuing the target company at 10x earnings and the acquirer at 20x earnings, then the acquirer is paying $10 for every $1 in earnings. If the market is paying $20 for every $1 of earnings for the acquirer, then the acquirer will buy the target, and pay 10x, and then have the market value the new Company ("NEWCO") at 20x. Thus it's accretive.

For example: Acquirer currently has $100 million in net income and 5 million shares outstanding, so the company earns $20/share. The market assigns a 20x P/E multiple. So each share is trading at $400/share.

The target has $100 million in net income and 5 million shares outstanding, so the target earns $20/share. The market assigns a 1x P/E multiple, so each share is trading at $20/share.

The acquirer buys the target at $20/share. They have paid 1x for every dollar of earnings. But then the market will (likely) value NEWCO at a P/E at 20x. So NEWCO will have achieved a large increase in valuation (assuming that the market values NEWCO at the acquirers previous multiple).

Obviously this is a very exaggerated example but the principle is the same: Deal is accretive if target's PE ratio is lower than that of acquirers.

Also, acquirers will always have to pay a premium to entice shareholders of the target company to sell. This is referred to as a Tender Offer. Usually Tender Offers are for 20%-50% above the current market price.

18) What is your greatest strength?

"My greatest strength is the ability to get things done quickly and accurately. Whenever I'm given a homework assignment I try to get it done as soon as it is assigned. Also, I make sure that I don't hand in anything without giving 100% effort and checking it over for errors."

This answer can be total bullshit; but they'll love it!

19) What is your greatest weakness?

This is a tough question to answer. You **never** want to give a real weakness. We're sharks and will ding you for the slightest perceived weakness. Instead, answer with the following:

"My weakness is a lack of experience. I feel that I'm well-suited for the position, however I lack the experience to substantiate my beliefs. As a result, all I'm really looking for is an opportunity to prove to you that I can do excellent work and become an integral member of the team."

Or, and perhaps even better because I think we're all guilty of this sometimes (especially bankers)

"My weakness is that I'm too hard on myself. Sometimes I need to take a step back and look at the big picture, instead of always focusing upon my mistakes. This leads me to sometimes not appreciate what I've accomplished, and instead only focus on my perceived errors."

20) Do "thank you" notes count?

NO, they don't. We decide right after we see you. But…**you should do it anyway because it makes you look good.** So, if you hit it off with one particular person and didn't wind up with the job, then perhaps you'll be able to keep in touch with this person. They DON'T help you, but they could hurt you if you don't send one so…. ALWAYS SEND ONE!! Here's an example below:

"Dear [Insert Mr or Ms. and then last name],

Thank you for meeting with me yesterday. I realize that you're very busy and appreciated the time spent to interview me. I feel that I could be a valuable asset to your team and would welcome the opportunity to produce good work alongside you. Thank you.

Best regards,

[insert your name here]

21) How should I dress and act while at work?

You should ALWAYS look your best. Dress in a suit. Seriously, it's very important. I wear $6 sweat pants from Wal Mart in which the string has broke and I have to utilize a safety pin in order to close the sweatpants, but.... work is ALL BUSINESS. You should ALWAYS shower, do your hair, put on cologne, wear a suit, have a pressed shirt on, a nice watch, etc. Treat EVERY day like an interview.

22) How should you act while at work?

Good question. You should ALWAYS be 100% business. Seriously, this may seem harsh, but… your colleagues are NOT your friends. You are paid a lot of money and you have to produce. If not, regardless of how much they like you, you will be fired. Oftentimes, late at night and on weekends, people get more comfortable around the office. Personally, I wear sweats and a t-shirt to the office on the weekends, but… my demeanor is ALWAYS 100% business. You need to get your work done, and have it done well, and then leave. When co-workers start throwing things around the office, or cursing, talking about girls, doing cocaine / Adderall in the bathroom to stay awake, your best bet is NOT TO PARTAKE! Everything in investment banking is 100% business, 100% of the time. Your colleagues merely have a false sense of security, but NO ONE IS IRREPLACEABLE. **DO NOT GET COMPLACENT**. I have seen so many people fired in this industry, usually because they become complacent and get lazy. You must ALWAYS have your guard up – at all times – and this includes company functions and drinks with your co-workers as well.

23) How to respond to the "Oh, you do investment banking? Cool, I have an extra $500 to invest. What do you recommend?"

I've been an investment banker for a while and I don't think my mother even knows what I do. She knows that I do investment banking, but she doesn't know what my job encompasses. Anyway, you're undoubtedly going to be asked the, "What should I buy?" question. You should answer as follows, "Actually, I deal with companies, both public and private, governments and things like that. Remember when AOL and Time Warner merged? Yeah, well we do things like that. We don't really get involved with the daily trading levels of the market."

Is this 100% accurate, NO! But…. is this "sort-of" right without making you look arrogant while also educating your friend a little? YES!!!!

24) Are Bankers Affected By the Daily Trading Levels of the Market?

In truth, we ARE affected by the daily trading levels of the market. Not on a grand scheme, but overall, we definitely are. For example, I remember back in 2004 and 2005 when Novamerican Steel appreciated from about $10 to ~$90 per share. EVERY Industrial banker was RUNNING after them and screaming "ISSUE EQUITY!!!!". Who the f*ck knows if that stock price won't crater to $20 a share? So… when it's at $90 a share, then the Company's equity is being priced very highly, and the Company should capitalize upon it. Also… in M&A transactions, Novamerican can utilize their higher stock price as **acquisition currency** in a deal. If they can get a company, or new shareholders, to accept their overpriced stock, then that's LESS NEW DEBT AND LESS EQUITY they'll have to issue in any new transaction.

Example: Imagine a $100 million transaction where I'm looking to purchase a Target company. If my stock is trading at $100 per share and I can get the Target to accept 750,000 shares, then I only need to worry about funding the remaining $25 million. This isn't EXACTLY right…. As oftentimes overpriced stock will be discounted and/or potential acquirers have to offer an acquisition premium (included in a Tender Offer) to entice shareholders to sell / trade in their shares, but…. in principle, this is generally right.

Another way in which trading levels influence financial activity is with Private Equity funds. In the private equity world, large variances in EV/LTM EBITDA valuations by the market allow for great LBO opportunities. In the Metals USA (MUSA) LBO by Apollo (a deal that I worked on – it sucked!!!!!!!!), MUSA was trading at 3.6x EBITDA while Reliance Steel and Aluminum (RS) was trading at ~7.5x. If I'm a private equity firm, I feel that I can capture some of that multiple variance and, hopefully, "flip" the company to another buyer, or in a secondary IPO for a higher multiple than the 3.6x that it was purchased for.

Private equity buyers usually pay less for private companies then they do for public companies because of a "liquidity discount". If a company is trading publicly, its stock can be bought and sold relatively easily in the public market. Public companies are accessible to almost everyone, practically anyone can purchase shares. Private companies have many less buyers. A lot more effort must be spent selling a private company: more diligence, management presentations, etc. Plus there are many less potential buyers to compete for the asset and bid up the price. As a result, private companies usually sell for ~20% less than Public companies. If a public company trades at 10x EV / LTM EBITDA, then a private company will sell, to a Financial buyer, for about 8x EV / LTM EBITDA. Strategic buyers usually pay a bit more due to the expected synergies, and also because they're not as focused on obtaining the absolute best purchase price.

25) Should I Work in an Industry or Product Group?

Product Groups (Leveraged Finance, Mergers & Acquisitions) vs. Industry Groups (Health Care, Industrials, etc.) is a huge debate. Personally, I don't think it matters much. You can learn a bit of everything in any industry or product group. Product Groups, especially M&A, tend to work harder and longer hours. However, your financial modeling skills in Product Groups tends to be better.

Again, I don't think it matters much.

26) Walk me thru the steps of a deal please....

No analyst will EVER be asked this in an interview, however Associates will.

First, there's usually a pitch, or a baiting process (banking is much like relationships). Either the targeted company sends out a Request for Proposal "RFP", so to speak, or makes it known that they want to sell themselves, or one of the senior bankers will receive word that there is a potential opportunity out there. Then the senior banker asks his analysts to create a pitchbook. The managing director will provide his insight but the analyst / associate normally creates most of the book.

The night before printing a book always sucks! Typically people make modifications until the 11th hour. Then you print and bind. Then the analyst/associate have to "flip" books to look for ANY mistakes. If there any "page changes" then you have to re-print and re-bind!!! It sucks! Ironically, I remember a few times being brainwashed and being so OCD that I would swap out a page even if it did not matter (i.e. if the color did not look sharp). It was like I was brainwashed to produce the highest quality work product regardless of the fact that my "improvements" were not necessary.

Anyway, your managing director goes to the pitch and hopefully wins. He may have to go to another round before being awarded the engagement – perhaps the targeted company wants to bring in 2-3 banks for "final rounds".

Lets say your investment bank has been awarded the business, lucky you!!!!! The senior banker will then negotiate the terms of the contract. The terms are usually a monthly retainer, plus a percentage of the final deal value, plus some incentives (xx% percent additional if you sell the company for over $XXXX million), plus the Company agrees to pay all reimbursable expenses in a timely manner.

Once the contract is signed, the investment bank divides up responsibilities. Typically, the bank has to create a selling memorandum, or a Confidential Information Memorandum ("CIM") and also create an online data room for diligence and to provide additional information.

The analyst and associate will likely create the selling memorandum. This takes about 3 weeks. These memorandums are usually 60-120 pages long and include overviews, financials, customer relationships, products, future prospects, etc.

During the creation of the Confidential Information Memorandum, another analyst will create a Diligence Request List and submit this to the Company. The Company will then send over, electronically or hard-copy, all of these items to the investment bank to help build the online data room.

Typical items on the diligence request list include: Company history, audits, internal financial statements, customer concentration information, human resources information, operations and technology information, etc.

The most common issue that I've seen during diligence is when a Company's financials are done on a cash basis vs. an accrual basis. If the CFO of the Company is not overly competent, then the Analyst / Associate can spend a lot of time creating documents for the online data room from "raw data" provided from the Company. It's not uncommon for an analyst, after spending 2-3 years as an investment banker, to be more competent than a CFO of a company, especially if the company is relatively small (under $100MM in annual revenue).

The Managing Director, Associates and/or Analysts will, at the same time, create a buyer's list for the Company.

The CIM creation is a collaborative process, with constant contact between the investment bankers and the client (AKA: company for sale, target, etc.)

Once the book is done, it is sent to the Company to proof, and then modifications are made, if necessary (typically very minor modifications). Then we print the CIM and distribute it to all potential buyers.

Prior to sending out the book, we make everyone who is going to receive a book sign a Non-Disclosure Agreement ("NDA"). Sometimes there's bickering with the language of the NDA, especially with private equity firms, but it eventually gets signed.

We then disseminate all the books, continue to build the online data room, and then we wait.

In the package that is sent to the potential buyers, we include a Process Letter that indicates when Indications of Interest ("IOI") are due. The Process Letter is essentially a schedule with due dates of how we will manage the Sale Process.

Once we send out the books, about ~3 weeks later we'll have all of the IOIs in our possession, then we decide who we want to bring back for Management Presentations.

While potential buyers are reviewing the book, the investment bankers, along with the Company's management team, create a Management Presentation. Typically a 1.5-2 hour Power Point presentation that tells potential buyers why this Company is so great.

The analyst and associate work on this, but senior bankers and the Company's management are more involved with this than usual. They coach the Management team to appear confident and feed them answers to questions that they believe will be asked (very similar to what this guide teaches – memorization and how to act the part).

Once the management presentation has been created (takes about 2-3 weeks – and typically it is set exactly at the IOI submission deadline), we then go thru the offers, and discuss with the Company who we will bring back for management presentations.

Once this is done, we inform the selected parties that they have been chosen for management presentations and the Company's management presents.

During this time, the data room will be completed; we use Intralinks.com and I've found them to be very good. A few days after management presentations are given, we grant access to the data room to everyone who has received a management presentation.

The potential buyers poke around and ask some questions in order to come up with a Letter of Intent ""LOI". LOIs are typically due about 2 weeks after the LAST management presentation is given.

The Company gives ~3-~9 management presentations, usually, so we would solicit LOIs from 3-9 parties.

Once the LOIs have been received, we narrow it down to 1-3 parties.

If one party expresses a ton of interest, we may sign an exclusivity agreement, meaning that, over the next 45-60 days, we will try to sell the Company only to this one buyer. Usually the terms of this agreement increases the probability that a deal is closed. If the target company has a lot of potential buyers, an exclusivity agreement will rarely be used.

Regardless of whether exclusivity is given, we then proceed towards "hardcore diligence". Lawyers get involved and the Company's CFO is basically GRILLED on the financials. Every month that passes, we have to send out "Updated Financials" and "Monthly Numbers" to see how the Company is tracking relative to its budget and plan. If it exceeds its numbers, then we will increase our purchase price, if it doesn't hit the numbers, then we reduce it. **If the Company really misses their numbers, then the buyers will likely walk and the Company won't be sold.**

An analyst or associate usually manages the diligence requests and also keeps a running tally of what was sent out and what was owed. The CFO usually has a VERY hard time during the 3-4 weeks of diligence and it's VERY hard for him to keep up with his daily responsibilities AND be on top of the diligence requests.

The point of diligence is to make the buyers feel COMFORTABLE!!! Once everyone feels comfortable and has no more questions then we proceed.

The investment bankers are ALWAYS trying to CLOSE the deal, so we usually try to keep the diligence timeframe within a month. If a request will take a long time, then we'll "push back" and tell the buyers that we're not going to satisfy their request. This happens sometimes if a buyer asks for something that we believe is not that relevant, will take too much time, and/or that potential buyer is falling out of favor and we want to proceed with other parties.

Once diligence is done, or, nearing completion, we, typically, whittle down the buyers to one, the chosen one!

Then we file documents to close the deal. The potential acquirer conducts "customer calls" with the Company's main customers to ensure that all relationships are strong, checking out if there are any "change of control provisions" – meaning that the Company will have to re-sign any contracts with customers if the Company is sold, etc.

Also, one of the last things decided upon is the level of working capital that is left in the business. The investment bankers want to get as much value for the Company as possible, so we want to take all the cash and equivalents off the balance sheet and have the buyers agree to a "normalized" level of working capital that is as low as possible – perhaps even negative. The buyers want it to be as high as possible cause, worst case scenario, they don't want to buy a company and then have this company come back to them one month later and say, "Hey, we need more money to fund our business!". The "normalized" level of working capital is ultimately a negotiation and both sides will eventually come to agreement if they want to get the deal done.

Once this is all taken care of, and the lawyers are satisfied, and the filings are done, we close! And then if the Company is nice, they send you presents! I once got a bottle of Cristal!

And then, 2 months later, you have a closing dinner to laugh about the deal and make nice!

Here are diagrams that we put together to explain the deal process timeline:

A combination auction *(targeted and controlled)* is the most appropriate strategy for XXXXXXX

XXXXXXX can structure this process to fit XXXXXXX's preferences

Strategy	Advantages	Disadvantages	Rationale
Preemptive sale *(One buyer)*	• Efforts focused on one buyer • Maximum confidentiality • Speed of execution • Minimum business disruption	• May not maximize value • Tied to result of one negotiation • Limited base of competition	• Reverse inquiry from logical "best" buyer with aggressive price • Clear sense of logical buyer • Limit damage from business disruption
Targeted auction *(2-8 buyers)*	• Speed of execution • Confidentiality maintained • Limited business disruption • Creates sense of competition • Avoids perception that property is being "shopped" • Reasonably accurate market test	• Requires substantial top-level management time commitment • Risks missing non-obvious buyers • Risk of impairing competitive bidding if key buyers exit process or show weak interest	• Allows for speed on execution with appropriate market test • Maintains confidentiality and limits business disruption • Enhances bargaining leverage • Clear sense of logical buyers
Controlled auction *(All logical buyers)*	• **Accurate test of market price** • **Formalized process** • **Creates strong sense of competition** • **Lower risk of excluding non-obvious buyers**	• **Requires substantial top-level management time commitment** • **Lack of confidentiality** • **May "turn off" logical buyers** • **Potential business disruption**	• **Provides balance between time, confidentiality and value** • **Enables competitive process** • **Large group of potential buyers**
Public auction *(All potential buyers)*	• **Heightens sense of competition among buyers** • **Finds "hidden" buyers** • **Full market test of market price**	• **Relatively long execution process** • **Greater risk of access to competitive information by "tire-kickers"** • **Highest risk of business disruption** • **Limited confidentiality**	• **Business is unlikely to be damaged by public process** • **Focus on maximizing shareholder value with no concern for time or confidentiality** • **Difficulty identifying buyers**

Sell-Side Auction Timeline

	–May	–June	–July	–August	–September
	–3 –4 –5	–1 –2 –3 –4 –5	–1 –2 –3 –4	–1 –2 –3 –4 –5	–1 –2 –3 –4

- Organizational Conference Call
- XXXXXXX Receives Off-the-Shelf Information
- XXXXXXX Onsite Due Diligence and CIM Creation
  - Receive Comments and Complete CIM
  - Review YTD Company Results
  - Complete Process Letter
  - Build Online Data Room
  - Buyer Calls/Negotiate NDAs
  - Distribute CIM and Process Letter
  - Prepare and Rehearse Management Presentations
  - Finalize Purchase Agreement
  - Indications of Interest Due
  - Management Presentations (Atlanta)
  - Grant Data Room Access
  - Distribute Purchase Agreement
  - Follow-Up Meetings
  - Q&A / Accounting & Legal Due Diligence
  - Final Bids and Markup of Purchase Agreement Due
  - Final Agreement and Negotiations Phase
  - HSR Filing and Approval
  - Announcement

- Controlled/Public Auction

2

Controlled/Public Auction Preliminary Timetable and Responsibilities

May								June								July								August								September						
S	M	T	W	R	F	S		S	M	T	W	R	F	S		S	M	T	W	R	F	S		S	M	T	W	R	F	S		S	M	T	W	R	F	S
	1	2	3	4	5	6						1	2	3								1			1	2	3	4	5								1	2
7	8	9	10	11	12	13		4	5	6	7	8	9	10		2	3	4	5	6	7	8		6	7	8	9	10	11	12		3	4	5	6	7	8	9
14	15	16	17	18	19	20		11	12	13	14	15	16	17		9	10	11	12	13	14	15		13	14	15	16	17	18	19		10	11	12	13	14	15	16
21	22	23	24	25	26	27		18	19	20	21	22	23	24		16	17	18	19	20	21	22		20	21	22	23	24	25	26		17	18	19	20	21	22	23
28	29	30	31					25	26	27	28	29	30			23	24	25	26	27	28	29		27	28	29	30	31				24	25	26	27	28	29	30
																30	31																				

−Month	−Description of Events	−Primary Responsibility
−May	−Kick-off organizational conference call	−XXXXXX X
	−Prepare information request list items	−XXXXXX X
	−Prepare company financial information\model	−XXXXXX X, XXXXXXX, AT
	−Collaborate and confirm buyer list	−XXXXXX X
	−Review requested information	−XXXXXX X
−June	−Begin preparation of CIM	−XXXXXX X
	−XXXXXX X on-site visit	−XXXXXX X, XXXXXXX
	−Complete draft of CIM	−XXXXXX X
	−Furnish comments on CIM	−XXXXXX X
	−Review YTD results / Greenlight next steps	−XXXXXX X, XXXXXXX
	−Confirm Process letter	−XXXXXX X
	−Begin calling buyers and negotiating confidentiality agreement	−XXXXXX X
	−Distribute CIM	−XXXXXX X
	−Finalize Intralinks index and begin constructing online data room	−XXXXXX X, XXXXXXX
−July	−Begin drafting management presentation	−XXXXXX X
	−Continue drafting management presentation	−XXXXXX X
	−Rehearse management presentations	−XXXXXX X, XXXXXXX
	−Finalize draft purchase agreement and assemble contract schedules	−LT, XX XXXXX
	−Finalize management presentations	−XXXXXX X, XXXXXXX
	−Indications of interest due	−XXXXXX X

XXXXXXX = XXXXXXX   **XXXXXX X = XXXXXXX LT = Legal Team**   **AT = Accounting Team**

Controlled/Public Auction Preliminary Timetable and Responsibilities

May								June								July								August								September						
S	M	T	W	R	F	S		S	M	T	W	R	F	S		S	M	T	W	R	F	S		S	M	T	W	R	F	S		S	M	T	W	R	F	S
	1	2	3	4	5	6							1	2	3							1				1	2	3	4	5							1	2
7	8	9	10	11	12	13		4	5	6	7	8	9	10		2	3	4	5	6	7	8		6	7	8	9	10	11	12		3	4	5	6	7	8	9
14	15	16	17	18	19	20		11	12	13	14	15	16	17		9	10	11	12	13	14	15		13	14	15	16	17	18	19		10	11	12	13	14	15	16
21	22	23	24	25	26	27		18	19	20	21	22	23	24		16	17	18	19	20	21	22		20	21	22	23	24	25	26		17	18	19	20	21	22	23
28	29	30	31					25	26	27	28	29	30			23	24	25	26	27	28	29		27	28	29	30	31				24	25	26	27	28	29	30
																30	31																				

–Month	–Description of Events	–Primary Responsibility
–August	–Select potential buyers for management presentation	–XXXXXX X, XXXXXXX
	–Management presentations in Atlanta	–XXXXXX X, XXXXXXX
	–Respond to questions	–XXXXXX X
	–Grant data room access	–XXXXXX X
	–Distribute purchase agreement	–XXXXXX X
	–Further accounting and legal due diligence	–XXXXXX X, XXXXXXX
–September	–Final bids and purchase agreement due	–XXXXXX X
	–Analyze, clarify and respond to final offers	–XXXXXX X
	–Negotiations with prospective buyer(s)	–XXXXXX X, XXXXXXX, LT, AT
	–HSR filing	–LT
	–Customer and buyer due diligence	–XXXXXX X, XXXXXXX
	–Finalize negotiations	–XXXXXX X, XXXXXXX, LT
	–Sign purchase agreement	–XXXXXX X, LT
	–Draft press release	–XXXXXX X, Buyer
	–Communicate transaction to employees, customers and suppliers	–XXXXXX X, Buyer

XXXXXXX=XXXXXXX   XXXXXX X=XXXXXXX   LT=Legal Team   AT=Accounting Team

4

Typical Day and Personal Confessions

Typical Day of an Analyst at a Bulge Bracket and Boutique Firm

I live 7 minutes from work, so I usually get up around 8:30 a.m. (living close to work is the BEST thing you can do) and stroll into work around 9:15-9:20. Since I'm not a morning person I'm fairly inefficient during the first few hours of the work day. I love the stock market, so from 9:30-10:00 I usually watch my stocks on Yahoo Finance if I don't have anything pressing to get done. Sometimes if I'm really tired, I'll leave work around 10 a.m., go home and then take a half hour nap before coming back.

From 11 a.m. – 6 p.m. I primarily do 2 things: satisfy the endless e-mail requests from my Directors (i.e. updating comps and send them to certain people, pull specific research reports, put together a Public Information Book ("PIB") on a company, do a one-page overview on a company, etc.). I usually get about 4-5 requests like this every day. They are totally unplanned and can strike you at any time. They take anywhere from 20 minutes to 3 hours to complete.

When I'm not answering these requests, I'm usually working on a pitchbook or a memo. With larger banks, whenever we are engaged on a transaction, we have to go to "commitment committee", an internal governing body that grants us approval to proceed with the transaction. In order to prepare for these committees, we need to compose a memo.

When I'm not working on memos or satisfying e-mail requests, I'm usually working on a pitch. This can take a long period of time, depending on how many pages I need to create – and how many I can just take from past pitches and recycle.

I don't eat lunch during the day, but many of the other analysts do.

Around 6 p.m. we eat dinner. Analysts are expected to order for the entire group. I don't use my corporate card, rather I use an American Express Blue Cash Rewards card. I figure that I'll put about $25,000 on my card per year. At 1.5% cash back, this works out $375/year just for using my card. Analysts are expected to keep all business-related receipts to submit reimbursement.

After dinner, I become super efficient. Sometimes I'll go to the gym from 8p.m.-9p.m. At night, I'm usually working on pitches and I scramble to get my work done as quickly as possible because I can't leave until I have everything done.

I'll talk to my parents and friends after 9 p.m. while I'm working. We all have headsets so I can talk and work at the same time.

At about 10 p.m. I start to look at the clock and begin to get slightly antsy to leave. Typically I'll leave at 11 p.m. on Monday – Thursday. If I don't have anything to do, I will still leave at 11p.m. because if I leave earlier, then my Directors may think that they are not giving me enough work to do.

When I have a lot to complete, or if I have to print books, I usually stay until at least 1 a.m. Printing books stinks because there are usually errors in them that I catch after they've been printed. When this happens, we do a page replacement in order to fix the error.

Typical Day at my New Firm (Boutique Bank)

I live 3 minutes from work so I usually get up around 8:15 a.m. and then get in by 9 a.m. I check my email and get to work. Throughout the day I'm working on information memorandums and financial models. I oftentimes hold conference calls with CFO's during the day as well to discuss the financial statements.

I travel a lot more now as well. Having been to Austin, Texas; Plymouth, Michigan; and San Francisco within the past 2 months (for business).

If I take lunch, I simply walk home and grab some food. I typically leave work around 9 p.m.

I work about 2-3 weekends per month and typically only 1 day per weekend. Nothing major. I like the boutique lifestyle significantly more than the "Bulge Bracket" life. However, to get into a boutique it is often necessary to "pay your dues" and go to a big name firm and spend a year or more there.

In fact, I would recommend that everyone strive to work for a Goldman, Citi, Morgan Stanley, UBS, BofA, etc. for a year and then quit after you get your bonus.

Personal Confessions

Summer of 2004 @ Large Bank

Basically, there are 2 reasons to do banking. The first is that you learn more in this industry than in many others (primarily because you're immersed in it, it becomes your life). You'll be in your early 20s and know more about the capital markets than 99.9% of the population. You'll also get paid well. 1st year analysts make $55,000 a year base and this year (2004), 1st year bonuses topped out at $45,000 ($65,000 in 2005). Out of the $100,000, you'll likely net around $52,000 after tax – not an overwhelming amount – but it's a lot for a 21-year old. Another advantage is that most of your meals are paid for. Dinner is paid for every weekday night (typical allocation is $25) and I get all 3 meals covered on the weekends if I go into the office. Black car service is also a plus. We can call a car and it will pick us up and bring us anywhere we ask. The only things I really pay for are rent, gym membership and spending money when I go out. So, monetarily, this job is very rewarding. Second year analyst's salary is bumped up to $60,000 and their bonus topped out this year at $70,0000 (2004). Third years get $65,000 base and topped out this year, bonus-wise, at $90,0000 (2004). First year associates get a base of $85,000 and their bonus is around $125,000. So you can theoretically be 25 years old and be making well over $200,000 a year.

The drawbacks about banking are the hours, I'm typing this at 8 p.m. on a Saturday and I've been here since 1:30 p.m. (I did just order $50 worth of sushi however – so it's not all that bad). I typically work from 9a.m. to 11 p.m. on Monday – Thursday, Friday from 9 a.m. to 8 p.m. I work about 2 Saturdays per month and usually I work 3 Sundays a month for about 7-8 hours. So, in total, I work about 80-90 hours a week.

Worse than the hours is the stress that goes along with the job. Your bosses will ask for things that just cannot be completed in the requested timeframe, and their response to you when you bring this up is, "Too bad. Find a way to get it done on time." Another stressful situation is when your boss is a jerk and asks for really obscure pages to be added to a pitch – and then right before you go to print he decides to take them out (so you wasted an entire day for nothing). This doesn't happen too often, however it's happened to a few of my co-workers.

Once I remember being asked to do a really difficult accretion dilution analysis with a lot of built-in covenants (leverage cannot exceed a prescribed multiple, merger has to be at least 10% accretive, include multiple synergy scenarios based upon the cyclical nature of the target's business, etc). I didn't know what to do and I remember calling my parents and being very stressed out. I was finally able to figure out how to properly run the analysis but I got about 2 hours of sleep that night (and I doubt they ever used the analysis).

Sometimes your bosses will be extremely vague and then make you feel like an idiot because you don't understand what they want. In these situations it's best to ask for clarification, however you don't want to ask too many times because then they'll think that you're not intelligent.

Today is October 29, 2004. Last week I was asked to do some difficult financial analysis. The problem was that I was also staffed to complete another book for a managing director. So I had two assignments – on a weekend. I got in on Sunday and the Director asks me how the book is coming along. I told him that I had to complete another book for a managing director. He didn't like this answer very much. His next e-mail to me said,

"When the F do you think we need to get this book done? Mark is leaving tonight."

This guy is probably the worst director I've ever worked for. Virtually all conflicts within the group involve him. My guess is that he has significant emotional problems in his life. He's the type of person that would go to the gym from 8 p.m. to 9 p.m. and then call a black car, come back to the office to grab his stuff and then take the black car home to NJ (while of course billing it to the client). Sometimes this guy doesn't even read my e-mails. I'll ask him a question such as, "Would you rather do this or that?" and he'll reply, "Yes".

I think he's bi-polar to be honest. He goes through these mood swings and I never know how he's going to act. Last week (mid-2004) he got upset because the printer ran out of paper while he was printing a document. Once he realized that the printer was empty, he screamed at all the analysts (in the analyst bullpen), "The next time this printer runs out of paper when I'm trying to print I'm taking $1,000 out of the analyst bonus pool." He can't do that anyway. He's a Director, so he has power. But not that much power. He'll be so nice to the managing directors, his bosses, but he'll treat analysts like they're nothing. I'll never be like him if I ever become a director. First off, my mood is relatively stable, and also I have more respect for others than he does. Analysts do work to benefit him; the least he can do is be appreciative.

I don't have much of a relationship with my directors. One is bi-polar, as previously mentioned, and another doesn't really like me. This guy doesn't like me because when I first started I wasn't a very good analyst. I was barely 21 and hadn't even graduated college at the time I started investment banking, nor had I gone through any Analyst Training Program. He's threatened to fire me and I think he questions my commitment and intelligence. In mid-2004 he asked me, "How does your weekend look?" I instantly knew that there was trouble brewing. He proceeded to staff me on a book that he demanded to see Monday afternoon. Want to know the real fucked up part? He staffed another analyst, the only one who's senior to myself, to "quality control" the book. That's like a slap in the face. This director and the other analyst have a good relationship because the other analyst is a loud-mouth and does a lot of work for this particular director. The other analyst is not very bright, (don't worry, I am dumb too), but I am smarter than this analyst so I took offense to the director's staffing of the other analyst to "quality control" the book. I hope this director does not detrimentally affect my compensation come bonus time (this was written in mid-2004). I have 8 months to change his perception, so in the long-run I'll be alright. However, at this moment, I'm the analyst he dislikes the most.

Fortunately, one of the other directors likes me a lot and thinks that I'm the best analyst in the group so that definitely helps. One of the associates really likes me too, he's really a quasi-director because he has strong relationships with many people in the business and has already brought in business. So basically I have 2 allies that will go to bat for me during bonus-time.

My social life has been pretty shitty since I started banking. The summer of 2003, when I worked at Morgan Stanley in their internal audit department, was great. I was hooking up with 5 girls at the same time and going out all the time. Fast-forward to this year, I'm hooking up with zero women on a consistent basis. I do have some great stories though. I hooked up with a former Miss Sweden in October 2004, she was visiting New York due to Hurricane Frances. She lives in Miami and looks like Cinderella. Actually, the first thing I said to her was, "Has anyone ever told you that you look like Cinderella". We kept in touch for 3 weeks, but she then stopped returning my phone calls. Just to say that I hooked up with a former Miss Sweden is good enough – though I would have liked to keep hooking up with her.

Besides that, I don't like Manhattan that much. I basically do the same thing every weekend, go out to clubs and bars.

It's now November 11, 2004. recently I've had to do a lot of financial modeling. I'm not very good at modeling and building in all the covenants that my bi-polar boss asked for. In industry groups, you do less modeling than you would in a product group. However, in M&A or leveraged finance, all you do is model, so you become extremely proficient in a short amount of time. In an industry group, you will learn a lot about your specific industry but not become as good a financial modeler as those in product groups. However, the more senior you become, the less important your financial modeling ability becomes.

In Industry Groups, if your boss asks you to do something very complicated, it's common to ask for help from more competent modelers (analysts and associates in M&A or Leveraged Finance). Overall, I would rather be in an industry group, primarily because the quality of life is usually slightly better. If you are in an Industry Group and are proactive in taking on financial modeling tasks, then you can learn how to become a competent financial modeler.

Recently, one of my associates did the model wrong and I had my director, the one who's bi-polar, call and scream at me. I don't really care if he yells at me because I'm doing the best I can and I already know that I'm a good analyst. But, I will mind if they make me assume responsibility for the model being wrong because I didn't build it. In banking they always want to make it seem like your job is not safe. They've made it clear that we get paid a lot to not make mistakes, so whenever a mistake is made then someone has to assume responsibility. As long as I don't get fired and get a nice bonus at the end of the year then I'm all set. Hopefully today's mix-up will not have any impact on my compensation and/or how my bosses think of me.

A girl was actually fired last week, after 3 months on the job. You have to be really bad to be fired from this job after 3 months. I know it's really hard to get an investment banking job, but once you're in, you should be set. Not many people get fired because it's not hard work after you've done something for the 100th time and it's easier to yell at someone, instill them with fear, and have them learn something than it is to fire someone and have to train a new person. That'll happen to me with the financial modeling, I'll get yelled at and have to spend about 100 hours learning how to become a better modeler, but once I do that I'll make fewer mistakes. So, your goal should be just to get a banking job. Once that happens you should be fine.

Two things bother me about this job. The stress and my lack of social life. The stress is bad and I regularly have to go into the bathroom and meditate because my life is extremely stressful. Sometimes if I leave work at 9 p.m., I am literally scared that they will call me back into the office at 1 a.m. and I won't get any sleep. I literally shiver when walking home "early" at 9pm because I'm scared that my Blackberry will go off. I guess that's something that I have to work on, but being 21 and already working in this industry for 9 months has conditioned me to be scared whenever I receive an e-mail from a boss (a boss is anyone who's been there longer than you). A 5 word e-mail can keep you in the office for the entire weekend.

My social life is also very shitty. I now meet girls online. I would prefer not doing that. I'm a good-looking kid (at least my mommy tells me so) and do meet girls when I go out, but I don't have time to ever follow-up with girls I meet at clubs/bars. So even if I hook up with them that night, we usually lose touch.

Weekend of November 19-22, 2004

This past weekend has cemented the fact that life as an analyst is about survival. If you can survive your time as an analyst then you'll be amply rewarded at the end. The problem is that no one cares about your time. On Friday I was told by my director that he would e-mail me on Saturday with a specific comp set. He didn't. So on Sunday he sends me this e-mail:

I did not hear from you on Sat and I had to leave at 2 today to head to las vegas for a dinner tonight. I finished reading the itron PIB as well as all the comverge materials and think I might have a better handle on what is going on in this market as well as locating some comparable companies that we can use in our presentation. I am hoping that you will have a faxed draft sent to my hotel by Monday morning Las Vegas time. I want to see the structure of the presentation as well as the status of the pages John outlined that he wanted on Friday. I am hoping that you spent some time this weekend preparing these. I will send another email with comps as I want to discuss them with John as I do not want to waste your time preparing stuff that ultimately will not be used.

Give me an update tonight when you get this. I will be landing around 9 EST or 6 PM Las Vegas time.

Regards

I like how he wrote, "I did not hear from you on Sat." Umm. YOU were supposed to e-mail ME and without your e-mail it's impossible to get any of the work done. I can't make up a comp set in an industry that I know nothing about. I told him this, in a nice way of course, and I was really scared that he was going to e-mail me back and have me work through Sunday night just to get him a draft for a pitch that is taking place on December 2. I would have been very upset, but he wouldn't have cared. My time means nothing.

Mid-December Update

It is now December 15, and my last 3 working weeks have been absolutely hell. I've been doing a lot of work for Apollo Management over that time span. Apollo is a private equity firm based in NY and they've asked for a complete and thorough analysis of the steel processor and service center industry. I've literally spent hundreds of hours putting together information for them and have produced about 100 pages of documents, including a 60 page book with about 140 graphs that I produced just for them. I feel like a whore. They ask for something in a 10 word email, and then I spend the next week putting it together. I've gotten about 4 hours of sleep a night over the past 3 weeks. On Monday night my body gave out on me. It was 1 a.m. and I just got hit with more Apollo work that'd have kept me there until 5 a.m – after working until 3:30 a.m. on Sunday night. My mind wouldn't cooperate and I couldn't do any work. I began to pace around the office and splash water on my face. My thoughts became jumbled and I could barely speak coherently. I walked up to my Associate and told him that I didn't feel well and then left. He sent out this e-mail, at 5:05 a.m. **(Yup, 5:05a.m. Crazy!)**

"David asked to leave at 1:30 tonight and was unable to continue working due to fatigue. I told him he could leave as it was clear he could not productively work. This put me and Rich in a great bind as we were responsible for turning and proofing the ASC OM that was sent to the client a short time ago. In addition, the analysis that Apollo was expecting to be sent tonight also had to be completed. Rich helped me with this and both have been sent to the respective clients.

I told David that I would be requesting an analyst change on this deal and that is what I am doing now. I am not comfortable with his ability to meet Apollo's extremely large requests for analysis in a timely manner."

When I woke up on Tuesday morning, I thought that I'd be potentially fired or, at the very least yelled at, because I left the office after my body broke down. However, only one person spoke to me about it and they said not to worry. Ironically, I'm still working on things for Apollo and was not taken off the deal team. Instead, it seems like they gave me a pass because they knew that I'd been killing myself for the past 3 weeks. I was very surprised that no one yelled at me about leaving – it's sort of like desertion during a time of war. But, I apologized to the Associate and now everything is back to normal. With everyone else overworked too, they simply swept my "desertion" under the table, acted like it never happened and did not mention it to the other analysts. Perhaps they wanted to preserve morale.

Hopefully things will improve over the next few weeks. They have to because things can't get any worse. Tonight is our company's holiday party, it's at Tavern on the Green in Manhattan. I'm pretty excited about the party because it means that I can get out of work at a reasonable hour! I'll go there to eat dinner, and then go home and sleep. The only bad part about the party is that my company does not hire a lot of women, so there won't be a lot of girls there. And even if there are a lot of women there, I don't want to hit on someone that works at my company.

(Inserted a day later) I didn't end up going to the party, instead I spent the entire night working on something for Apollo. Fun times in investment banking (notice the sarcasm).

Another Update – January 2005

Wow, I have a major update to provide. We moved to a new building in Midtown. It is a tremendous upgrade over our previous work-space, the cubes are bigger and the office is brand new. It's literally amazing.

Also, I finally got transferred to a new group! I originally worked in the industrials group, we were one of the top banking groups in the bank; held in very high esteem because we got a lot of deals done. However, with this reputation comes a lot of hard work. We put in very long hours. Over the past 2 months, I would work until about midnight on average – with many days having me get out at 3, 4 and 5 a.m. I also usually worked 7 days a week and was staffed on 3-4 deals at the same time.

Because we did so many deals, we got a lot of leeway too. And my behavior started to change, I began doing things that I now regret and am not proud of. Not only did I begin coming into work later (around 9:30a.m. or 9:45a.m.), not shave every day, and sometimes wear the same clothes from the day before, but I also began more lavish in my expenses. Nothing crazy, like going to strip clubs on the Company's tab; but I began charging weekend meals even when I wasn't in the office, expensing taxi cab receipts on the way to clubs, drinks at clubs, expensive dinners with women, etc. My Directors never questioned any expense and everything was approved. Again, I am not proud of my behavior, but it's important to disclose that when people are stressed and overworked, the ability to resist temptation decreases.

Additionally, I would also use black car service as the personal chauffeur for my girl friends. Friday and Saturday nights, if I wanted to see you, then I'd send a car to pick you up from New Jersey, Westchester, Long Island, Brooklyn, Queens, etc. I remember bringing this girl from LI over to my house at 4:30 a.m. Good time in investment banking (not sarcastic!).

Then, the next morning, I would send them back using black car service. They loved it. And… I loved it too ☺ I live within walking distance of work so I rarely ever used car service for myself, rather I always used it for my girls.

During Christmas time my asshole director (the bi-polar one) came over to me and said, "uh hummmmm...as homework I need you to update all of these steel precedents and also do one pagers for each transaction." I hate this guy and have no respect for him – he didn't even thank me for cranking out that 60 page book that I did for Apollo that kept me in the office until 4 a.m. for practically 2 weeks straight.

So like most things I do for him (since he would oftentimes ask for something one week and then not follow-up / ask for it once it was completed), I put it off and waited for him to ask me about it. He never did ask me about it so I thought it wasn't a top priority. Then a week later, he comes up to me and says, "Where are the overviews?" I told him that I didn't have them done. He screamed at me and said that I "fucked" him. That was bad.

A few days later I got extremely tired at 9:30 p.m. and couldn't focus on doing anymore work. I was given a lot of work to do at 9:15 p.m. that would have kept me there until 2a.m. So, instead of doing it, I dropped it off in the word processing department and then went home. My associate sent me an e-mail on my Blackberry but I was sleeping, and then he called my cell phone but…. I was sleeping. The next day, he called me over and said that I should never do that again and that he was there until 2:30 a.m. getting my work done. I felt really bad because this associate really does a lot of work. Most associates just dump on the analysts, but he doesn't. He works just as much, if not more, hours than the analysts and he also does a tremendous amount of work – plus he's a cool guy. So I felt bad.

Both of these incidents happened within a week of each other. Ironically, I actually got like 8 of the 12 steel processors precedent transaction overviews done and then chose not to give it to my director. I was content with waiting another day or two and handing him all 12 at once. This was a bad strategic move as well.

Back in June, I met with human resources and requested to change groups within the bank. The bi-polar Director was very disrespectful to all the analysts and associates. It didn't bother many of them that much, but it bothered me. I always had a sense of pride and never felt that I was inferior to anyone. This conflict, combined with working more hours than most groups within the bank, led to my request for a transfer to another investment banking group. My group denied my request, indicating that I was "too valuable" and stating that they lived through my first two months, when I sucked, and wanted to benefit from my work now that I was productive.

Since that time in June, once the request was denied, and the Managers in my group knew that I wanted out, things were a bit weird, perhaps they felt that I was not fully committed (which was true).

Anyway, after those 2 incidents in December ("fucking" my Director with the overviews and leaving work to sleep), things started to change. That whole week I wasn't getting any new work. And, what made things really suspicious was that deals that I was previously staffed on were being re-staffed with other analysts. I knew that something was up. Then on Thursday at 3:30 p.m. I received a phone call from HR and they requested that I attend a meeting at 4:30 p.m. I knew this wasn't good.

I went to the meeting and was informed that my group doesn't want me anymore and that I had to interview for a position in the Financial Restructuring Group, and that if I don't get it I will be fired.

This was not a good meeting. I was shocked. I was scared. And I thought that I might be fucked too. I wanted to switch groups, but I wanted to switch groups because I didn't like my group, not because the group didn't like me. My old group kept telling me that they would not let me go, that I was "too valuable", now they're telling me that they don't want me? WTF?

Dinner was weird that night with the group that fired me. I didn't say anything, and then after dinner I walked into the Group Leader / Head Managing Directors' office and thanked him. He said that he was sorry that things didn't work out and that hopefully they'll work out in Financial Restructuring. He's a really good person. Very kind and respectful of everyone. I then spoke to the director who doesn't like me, not the director that I have no respect for and who's an asshole (bi-polar one), rather just the one that doesn't like me. I have a lot of respect for the Director that doesn't like me because he's smart and puts in a tremendous amount of hours. He recently had a kid and he's still working until 11 p.m. every night, except Friday, and he usually works on Sunday too. We spoke and he said that it "just looked like I didn't care". That he knew I was bright enough and that I had potential but that I didn't care enough. Then he brought up what happened with the other bi-polar Director and also how I screwed my Associate over. I had nothing to say. I asked for his advice on how I can prevent this from ever happening again and he said that I should always give 100% effort at all times, regardless of whether I like the person or not.

On Friday, I went to my desk with the group that fired me and waited to be interviewed for the restructuring job. It turned out that the guy who was going to interview me was traveling and that he'd have to interview me on Monday. I wasn't doing anything at work on Friday so I left at 3 p.m. I didn't say anything to anyone, I was embarrassed, and just left.

That weekend was the toughest weekend of my life. I got extremely depressed every single day and had a panic attack on Saturday night. I literally was crying on my bed, in a fetal position, with a racing heart and couldn't breathe. I think I had a mental breakdown. It was really scary. I then took a shower and went out to Crobar with like 15 friends. I went to a Knicks game on Sunday and was so depressed that I just wanted to go home. I looked online for psychiatrists because I knew that this could not continue. I actually saw one today for the first time, he was really cool. I felt better. Anyway, I interviewed on Monday at 11 a.m. with Restructuring. I was only supposed to meet with a few people but I met with the entire team. They were so nice and I made a very good impression – I wrote this primer, so I'd hope that I'd interview well. They asked me no finance questions, rather it was all geared towards, "tell me about industrials and why things didn't work out and how do we know that things will work out here." I had an advantage because I DID do good work in industrials, when the restructuring guys called up my past bosses and asked them if I'd do a good job and had questions regarding my work quality, my old bosses stood by me and said that I was a good worker and that I'd succeed (I'd actually asked to leave Industrials as early as June 2004, but they wouldn't let me go. So my bosses all knew that I was miserable in my previous group, but I still managed to bang out quality work).

I thought that they'd let me know right there, but they told me that they'd call me back that night or the following morning. The past weekend and that night I realized how EVERYTHING I AM is connected to my job. Everything I buy, everything that I do for women, my social life, even the health insurance that my shrink is a member of comes from my job. I got depressed again and went to bed early.

I woke up early to see the psychiatrist again, he was really cool (again). Then I went home and basically worried about my job. I watched a bad movie and called my parents and then my phone rang. The HR woman informed me that restructuring wants me. I thanked her for giving me this opportunity, told her that I was felt fortunate because many others would have just been fired and that I can assure her that I will become an excellent analyst. I'm actually writing this from the new computer in my new group.

The only thing that I don't like about my new group is that they're a lot more strict on expenses. I could, and did, push through literally anything while in Industrials and would get promptly reimbursed. I'd get like $3,000 expense checks. This group is a lot more strict and I'll likely be getting $300 expense checks.

I've already spent a few days in restructuring and I've done absolutely nothing constructive. There has been no work. I've looked at some past pitches and restructurings of steel companies, since I understand that space really well, and felt as if the pitches in industrials were a lot more difficult and complex than the pitches in Restructuring. In general, my work in industrials was a lot harder, and there was a lot more work, then there will be here. I literally left yesterday at 6:30 p.m. and I don't think that I'll have to come in many weekends. I may actually be able to have a life!!!! I went from working in the group that has the most stress and worst hours in the bank, to working in a group that has the best hours and least stress in the bank – and I'm getting paid the same amount.

The only problem is that we were busy in industrials because we had a lot of deal flow. We don't have nearly as many deals in restructuring, which worries me because if you don't produce in banking, then you're gone. But, I'm going to enjoy my new group, and my free time, and because I came from industrials I can literally get work done faster than many of the other analysts in the bank (I had to if I ever wanted to go home). Good times in investment banking.

Summary

In the interview, above all else I would stress that you're willing to work hard, that you know that banking is tough and that it's not for everyone, but that you're willing to work hard, are eager to learn and that you'll do whatever it takes to get the job done.

MOST IMPORTANTLY. HAVE CONFIDENCE THAT YOU CAN DO THE JOB. Don't be conceited. Just be confident and KNOW that you can do the job. If you sincerely know that you can be a good banker and put up with all the bullshit that I talked about, then you will get a banking job.

Remember, CONVINCE THE PERSON THAT YOU'RE INTERVIEWING WITH THAT YOU'RE A PERFECTIONIST AND THAT YOU CAN DO THE JOB!!

A good book to read, which really helped me get my current job is **Ask the Headhunter by Nick A. Corcodilos**. I recommend that everyone read this.

If you love this guide and believe it contributed to your ability to land a job, increase your signing bonus, etc. Feel free to spread the love or make a voluntary contribution to show your thanks and appreciation! You can email me at davejaffee@gmail.com

www.ingramcontent.com/pod-product-compliance
Lightning Source LLC
Chambersburg PA
CBHW081245180526
45171CB00005B/547